Live Music Therapy,
Audible Pure Tones

The Productive Use of Sound and Singing
An Emotional Self-Doctoring Yoga

Published by Live Music Therapy Press
Star Rt. Box 379-A Burnet, Texas 78611

First Printing 1988

ISBN 0-9620269-1-3

When my thoughts and emotions are making me unhappy, I take time out and sing myself a get well song. I sing about the way I truly want to be and that helps me let go of the other stuff - the unevolved ways of being that do not help.

Live Music Therapy helps me close the gaps between the attitudes I still allow and the attitudes I'd rather have be more full-time and full-spectrum. One of my biggies is impatience. I have quite a few songs I remind myself with. There is one from the movie Brother Sun, Sister Moon:

> "If you want your dream to be, build it slow and surely,
> Small beginnings, greater ends, heartfelt work grows
>   purely.
>
> If you want to live life free, take your time go slowly.
> Do few things but do them well, simple joys are holy.
>
> Day by day, stone by stone, build your secret slowly
> Day by day you'll grow too, you'll know heaven's glory."

For letting go of the past I often sing "Dawn Chorus" by David Spangler and Milenko Matonovic:

> "Morning comes and I greet the dawn,
> I'll take the day as it comes along
> Yesterday has been and gone, I'm spreading my wings
>   today!
>
> I'll not be caught in my history,
> The past shall have no hold on me,
> Exploring a new possibility, I'm making a brand new day!"

For letting go of another person I often sing, "I Release You" by Michael Stillwater:

> When we release this world we find
> Heavenly peace surrounding our mind.
> When we release this world we find
> Heavenly peace and people so kind.

I release you, you release me.
Now we are happy,
Now we are free
Now we are just like God made us to be."

When I need some attitudinal inner strengthening it may take me a little while to get into the song, to get to where it starts to energize me and starts to sound good. When I do get into it, it really boosts my energy level. Compensating for off-center thoughts and emotions with some energetic expression of the on-center values I desire in my life, is a way to freshen up my consciousness and exercise the singer in me. This approach is what I call hands-on live music therapy.

I can skip feeling sorry for myself, or impatient, or selfish, or whatever, by substituting a song that speaks to feeling grateful for myself, or patient, or giving, or whatever. I get busy tuning into a spirited song and it's real easy to leave that old me stuff behind. Most of the time I am feeling grateful for myself and patient and giving, but not all of the time. Singing my ABC's of emotional wellness keeps me on line, closer and closer, to full time basis. I have studied lots of recorded music to find suitable songs for my personal repertoire of healing and wholeness songs. I know many songs for each of the valuable attitudinal qualities I want to be expressing in my life.

Over the years I have filled up notebooks with the songs I have learned about forgiveness, communion with nature, humility, sharing, rebirth, release, being present, being gentle, being loving, and so forth. I have utilized these songs from diverse sources, including some original songs and chants, for tuning into a higher consciousness and integrating a higher consciousness.

The medicine I am taking when I am ill attitudinally is a double layered thing. I get the word meaning of the lyrics and I get the sounding treatment of expressing myself. The value therapeutically and spiritually of making sounds has been well known for thousands of years. In the many cultures of the world there have been many teachers and healers who have demonstrated and taught how we can use what is, in a single word, best described as toning, to energize ourselves and cure ourselves. Laurel Elizabeth Keyes' book *Toning, the Creative Power of the Voice*, is one helpful guide.

A low, deep, full sound will energize me physically when I need a boost. Various kinds of sounds can be used to help us stay centered and alert. The value of toning can be included in singing. In doing this I usually slow the song down and resonate thoughtfully and *sound-fully* some of the notes that appeal to me. Usually these notes are where the word meaning is also peaking. In the middle of a song which I am singing for its heartfelt value and for the toning exercise, I can, with a deep breath, take one note, and one word, way out in fullness, like an Om.

I also consider toning to mean toning the consciousness through the word meaning of the lyrics. I sing to change poor behavior patterns and impure thoughts. I sing to reinforce the positive values I desire to integrate and express on a more full-time basis. And I sing to exercise the soundmaker in me and derive the benefit from the sounds. I also like to Om and I like to use other toning frequencies. My point is that live music therapy will work for us in both ways, healing through sound and through meaning.

I can provide live music therapy for other people also. Listening to what my friends and family members, or clients, are expressing, and watching their behavior, I can reach out to them intuitively and line up a song in my mind to sing to them. Or sometimes just make one up on the spot.

Live music therapy can come forward thoughtfully or spontaneously. It might be just a very short song or chant that can be repeated. As I repeat something I can feel the meaning sink in deeper. I can hear myself come more into alignment with the truth of the lyrics and more into alignment with Singing Me. Singing Me is a part of me I enjoy very much.

This book defines Live Music Therapy/Audible Pure Tones, the productive use of sound and singing. It explains how this emotional self-doctoring yoga will help us grow. The productive use of sound and singing is something we never cease to derive benefit from. I do not see how anyone could ever be finished with this subject. As far as we have come, we still have that much further to go. The following material will help many of you, I hope, get started or keep going. And, to some extent, it will help explain why you would want to.

The methodology is already in us. This book is simply showing the way to what we each already have, although it may be latent, and can assist to bring the sleeping methodology awake. We need to meet the information presented with some initiative. Your own experience of sound and singing will be your best guide, and while you are raising up what is latent-in-you to become what is manifesting-in-you, this book is your friend.

Live Music Therapy is a live moment to moment yoga. It works best as a healing response to unproductive moods and is best utilized in a spontaneous way. The actual sounding expression is normally centered around a sung affirmation, with or without instrumental accompaniment. The song may be improvisational, originating in the emotional context of the moment, or a known song that fits the emotional context of the moment. Part of a song, perhaps just one line, may be all that is needed. Often too, the whole song will be used. Live music therapy need not be restricted to expressions which are entirely or part vocal. Live music therapy can be entirely instrumental, but in respect to the general discipline which will be described on the following pages, which is a process of balancing the emotions, the use of the voice is the primary consideration.

Live music therapy - LMT, is a ritual of cleansing. The release of the unloving element is prepared for in the attraction to the loving song: hearing it, repeating it. The singer creates impact because the tools of making sound are combined with the tools of the emotions. The live music therapist uses empathy to guide the intuition. She[1] knows that to provide treatments she must be in touch with the emotion the song's phrases and melody minister to. Being sensitive to the emotions in another person or couple, or group, the LMT practitioner is grounded in the moment, and this is what it takes for beautiful sounds to come forward and be healing.

A bell, a drum, a flute, a voice, a waterfall, a rainstorm, the hum of a sailboat, the whisper of the leaves, the wail of the wind, the rolling on of the waves, the echo in a cave, the reverb, the timbre, the tone ... the world of sound is a very rich and diverse place. The expressive energies of live music therapy are not seeking to be musical so much as to just be resonant. What precedes music, what music is built on, and what is part and parcel of live music therapy,

---

[1] I have taken the liberty to do something a little different in respect to third person pronoun usage. Live music therapy is for men and women and male readers should read "she" as meaning she or he, just like female readers have done when he or she is condensed to "he."

is the *indwelling* beingness of sound, Audible Pure Tones. The body of sound we experience in music healing activities is composed of audible pure tones. A complete piece of healing music may consist of just one audible pure tone. The priority of live music therapy as an expression of sound is to activate the native, individual, toning powers. From the pure and simple tone resonating joyously for itself, the body of sound effortlessly expands into the various movements of musicality.

Audible Pure Tones - APT, is the outward and inward experience of the multi-dimensional, omnipresent reality of Sound. We hear pure sounds in nature. We hear pure sounds in voices and instruments. We hear pure sounds in meditation.

> Silence is the most ancient of cures.
> It is the building up of vital elements
> And it is the antidote for a system that is leaking.
> Silence is singing with the mouth closed.

The sensory goal of quiet meditation is the activation of the inner ear. The pleasure of silence is brought forward in currents of Sound. Vocal expression is centered in hearing the melody inwardly before it is let go in outward song. Hearing is the key to both passive and active arts. The place of the consummate artist is consummate receptivity.

Whatever you call it, healing with sound and music is an emotionally and spiritually vitalizing form of exercise. Whatever you call it, the question is, of course, are you doing it? If you are, the empowerment will be working for you. The purpose of this yoga is to clear negative emotions and build positive emotions. Channels of higher communication are opened as we purify the emotions and strengthen the auditory receptors. The heartfelt context is the biggest live aid to working soundmaking exercises to best advantage. The heart *chakra* is just below the throat and ear *chakra*. Emotional advantages work directly for you on the musical level. This is why live music therapy is a household science, that is, having to do with family. The LMT part is more the emotional exercise and emotional healing part. The APT part is more the transcendental meditation part. Both LMT and APT stand by themselves as wholeness progress methods, but because they are always overlapping and because wholeness is the goal we are all working towards, it seems clearer to call the whole discipline Live Music Therapy/Audible Pure Tones or LMT/APT. Emotional exercise and healing generate mystical perceptions. Experiencing your tone inwardly and making your tone outwardly certainly do benefit the emotions.

To get started with LMT/APT do these things:

One. Make a daily routine of making just pure sound; no melody or words. Let your tone come forward. Take a couple deep breaths. The sound will come. Om, Hu, Ra, and others are traditional sounding syllables. Whatever you do enunciate while toning, try to make it a full and resonant sound. Do it patiently, lovingly, and with interest in what can be heard when we relax mentally and nourish the auditory sphere of consciousness.

Two. When you are getting out of balance emotionally or another member of the household is, make up a song or sing one you know, something to regain positive momentum for the emotions. Often just a simple chant or a few special lines of a song will do nicely. Repeating it several times will further anchor the mood reversal.

The course of instruction is very short. Really, it is too simple for words. It can be sensed more directly than it can be explained. Hearing is the single best verbal clue. Breathing is the second best clue. Soundmaking needs air. Third is vowel; to vow, to declare. The vowel makes up the intonational language of toning as a base derivative. Ma, Ra, Va, it is A. Om or Joy it is O. The vowel is the enunciation of an unimpeded sound. The mouth stays open and the toning exercise is free to expand in duration, fullness, and resonation, to the extent the breath permits. The basis in speech and sounding of any vow, declaration, affirmation, of any enunciated word, is the vowel. It is the open passageway of sound. Fourth is word content, the meaning. There are words that can describe the Om or other toning frequencies to give us a verbal background of what the syllable symbolizes, what it invokes, and the whys and hows of it being to our advantage to utilize. Toning exercises can be worked through everyday words listed in the dictionary. Home and Joy are good ones. He, Key, She, Be, We, Thee, can carry a high vibration E intonation. The word level adds another dimension of meaningfulness to the sounding practice.

A nice progression is to start with the pure vowel, for example, O, and gradually round it out into an Om. As the Om becomes full and resonant, you have what you need to make a convincing Home or Joy. The righteous toning of one word is a nutritious basis for evolving a chant. A chant is a group of words that make up a statement. Chanting is a potentizing delivery system for affirmations of desired changes and progressions. A chant is repeated open-endedly until the sensory and sensing experience is complete. When the desired level of conviction is thoroughly resonated in us, we will be satisfied emotionally and the exercise may be said to be complete. It is the repetitive nature of chanting that makes it such a powerful tool for cleansing and transformation. A sentence or two from a song can be used for chanting. The important thing is this: the successful practice of LMT/APT is based on repetition.

We train our bodies through regular exercise. By stretching muscles regularly we train them to keep limber. We also can train the emotional body to stay supple and maintain an alignment of positivity. By one-liners, chants, whole songs, and tonings, we pull the emotional difficulties - the doubts, the angers, the inertias, the impatience, the carelessness, and so forth, into positive alignment. The force of transmutation we utilize in the yoga of Live Music Therapy is the Sound Current and the Power of the Word. LMT is both a sensory therapy and a therapy of understanding. Parts of songs, chants, and whole songs can be used as declarations which treat a negative pattern of consciousness with its antidote, a corresponding positive pattern of consciousness. When we sing our affirmations we literally resonate the substantive energies of chosen beliefs into ourselves cellularly. Through live sound and heartfelt musical expression we bathe ourselves in the vibrations of desired ideals. The big practical payoff of this joyous discipline comes in the everyday actions that become increasingly more integrated with the purifying principles our live music therapy lyrics speak to. Singing and toning our way through negative straits necessarily engages the transformative energies of the heart. The heart is close to the vocal center and it is the master organ. It is what rows us through evolution. Releasing these extremely hopeful energies through the throat produces waves of positive alignment. The doubt departs. The anxieties and inertias disappear. By learning to take hold of negativity by the horns, and through willing and honest confrontation, lift ourselves, we are no longer plagued by depression and inconsistency. With practice, negativity simply becomes the raw material that is directly fed into the transmutation process of live music therapy yogically practiced and lived out.

There is always a transference going on in the quality of life between the emotional and physical levels. Emotional exercise is expressed in many ways and what it all comes down to is loving. Loving comes from understanding and vitality. Being centered emotionally becomes natural when the mind and body are in balance. When we use our reason to perpetuate fraud on the emotions, the mind is out of balance. There is no reason at all to deaden hurt feelings. In the first place, they don't really die and, secondly, it's far better to face the difficult moment when it is present. Otherwise we are, by habit, caught emotionally in the past, trying to discover what went wrong.

The body's essential desire is for breath. To increase the oxygenation of the blood, we increase the amount of oxygen coming into the lungs by quickening the breath and/or deepening it. Whereas physical inertia and emotional contraction may be mended with a simply derived enlargement of oxygen, nervousness is mended by somewhat subtler attention. When there is a constriction in the inhale or exhale, in the natural rise and fall of the breath as it enters and leaves the body, there is an associated pattern of nervousness in our physical movements and behavior. The constriction needs to be relaxed and released. By watching the breath and following its course, and visioning each new breath passing effortlessly by the constricted area (be it in the abdominal region or in the chest), on its way in and on its way out, we consciously reclaim a smoother pattern of breathing. When the breath is natural we are predisposed to the natural rhythm and the nervous system comes into balance.

By making connections between body and emotions, body and mind, and mind and emotions, the healing energy is found. Now we rebirth by breath, now by sound, now by touch, now by quiet reflection, now by dynamic release ... When we feel good loving is very natural. When we feel a little less than our best, it is surprising how unnatural it may seem.

There is so much delight in the world of sound and hearing. You might be cruising the waters in a wooden sailboat and the hull starts to hum. You might be cozily indoors hearing the rain on the roof. That same metal roof might be making different sounds on a rapidly warming sunny morning. Or hearing from the crickets and cicadas at evening, or the birds in the morning; all expressing just for the pleasure of being part of Creation. Spirit sings to us and through us in a multitude of ways. If we feel poorly we do LMT/APT to lift ourselves. If we feel frisky we do it to keep on course. If we are stuck in a rut and frustrated we do it. The Live Sound of Universal Love Energy is the central and core process God uses to sustain Creation. God makes us to sing. We, like the rest of Creation, are Sounding Instruments.

It is not necessary to do these exercises in any certain way or schedule, although this sure may be a helpful place to begin. It is kind of difficult to totally define and conceptualize this yoga, other than to say, either you are doing it or you are not. To know whether you are doing it is to be aware of the benefits. To be able to utilize your voice as needed to supply the right inflection[1] and the right reflection,[2] is to be productive in the sound-wise and heart-wise science that protects the family from ruts of negativity.

The use of sound can be interwoven into the day to help keep your energy up and your attitude clean and productive. It always corresponds to the lighted way when used in this way. To be at your best for the working service of being a mother, a father, a builder, a gardener, a teacher, a whatever; the better your mood, the better things get on. You can enrich your creative atmosphere with loving and empowering vibrations by making your loving tone throughout the music. This is an energetic way to ward off the evil spirits of laxity, fixity on wrong things, and irreverence (irrelevant thoughts and speech). Laxity is from overmuch inertia and leads to ineptitude. Fixity on wrong things is emotional stubborness and leads not to sanity. Irreverence leads to temptation. We discern the area of disharmony and give treatment. If it is laxity we find a tune that stimulates movement physically and activates the breath; if it is fixity, a tune that bespeaks the flow of love to make change and reach out for understanding; if it is irreverence, a tune that cleanses the perception and clarifies the direction. For laxity sing about movement, for fixity sing about moving on, and for irreverence, sing about moving on course.

In LMT/APT we use a lot of silence and breath to get centered. We might also use a chart of various chants and parts of songs to have as a selection tool in improvising our sessions. We might make use of places that offer interesting and helpful acoustical

---

[1]Modulation of the voice in speaking; any change in the pitch or tone of the voice in singing.

[2]The turning of the mind to that which has already occupied it (remembrance); the result of attention or continued consideration.

effects, like domes or archways. Just a small piece of three foot diameter sewer pipe does nicely, making an overtone that goes round and round. There are lots of possibilities for expanding an LMT/APT practice. The main thing is you know where your emotions are hiding. Live music therapy works with you to open the knots. We feel better. That is why we do it. And that is why we keep doing it.

A live music therapy treatment chart can be made. For example:

Blockage	Antidote/Liberating Lyrics	Source
anxiety	"Let it Be"	Beatles
self-abstraction pride preoccupation with externals	"It's a gift to be simple, It's a gift to be free It's a gift to come down Where we are to be And when we come down To the place just right We will be in the valley Of love and delight. When true simplicity is gained To bow and to bend We will not be ashamed Turning and turning Will be our delight Till by turning and turning We come round right"	traditional Shaker
preoccupation with past and/or future	"This moment is different from any before it This moment is different, it is now ... If I don't kiss you that kiss is untasted I'll never, no never, get it back But why should I want to I'll be in the next moment Sweet moment, sweet lover, sweet life ... The air that you breathe is different From any before it, it is now!"	Incredible String Band

shallow or constricted breathing	"Breathing, all creatures are Brighter than the brightest star You are by far You come right inside of me Close as you can be You kiss my blood And my blood kiss me."	Incredible String Band
disinclination to sing	"If you want to sing out, sing out And if you want to be free, be free Cause there's a million ways to be You know that there are, You know that there are."	Cat Stevens
tightness self-conscious-ness	"Education is all around It's in Light and it's in Sound Make your way through the universe Sing and dance, no need to rehearse"	original

contractedness separation	"Happiness runs in a circular motion
	Life is like a little boat upon the sea
	Everybody is a part of everything
	   anyway
	You can have it all if you let
	   yourself be."
		?

sleeping late inertia	"Why sleep when the day has been
	   called out by the Sun
	From the night cause the Light is going
	   to shine on everyone
	Why sleep when sleep only closes
	   up our eyes
	Why sleep when we can watch the
	   Sun rise?
	We were meant to see the beginning
	   of the day
	I believe it was planned to lift us
	   this way
	Take you an apple and take you a song
	And watch a baby day be born."
		Melanie

introverted self-obsession	"Brother Sun and Sister Moon I seldom see you, seldom hear your tune Preoccupied with selfish misery Brother Wind and Sister Air Open my eyes to visions pure and fair That I may see the glory around me"	"Brother Sun, Sister Moon" (movie)

Fitting toning exercises into all that we do makes us what we can be. Transmitters. Singing to sunsets, sunrises, birds, sisters and brothers of all kinds - it makes a transmitting, and isn't it fitting to play our parts in the cosmic symphony? Music and massage, music and art, music and gardening, music and exercise, music and whatever; if it is healing it is going to have a good input on the other activity. If it is live and healing it is going to have an even greater effect. No matter what you have had or have not had in the way of musical education, the fact remains that we are all musicians. Melody and rhythm are at least latent potentials in every person. You breathe it, you feel it, you sing it; no thinking necessary.

Laughing is a form of LMT. When the emotions release and sounds are made, a music arises that is healing to self and others. Joy permeates the voice because sorrow has been released. No matter how well we may seem to be doing emotionally, indeed, no matter how well we are actually doing; there are always bits and pieces of negativity floating around and being retained. That is to say, there is always room for improvement emotionally. Happiness can keep stretching by further and further release of unloving and unliving bits of mood and consciousness. Whenever there is full belly laughter there is a healing release happening. No matter how well you were feeling before, after a bout of unrestrained laughter you will be feeling better.

You can use the hands to bring out your live music therapy as though you were conducting, conducting forth the sounding joy from self. You can use the feet to generate some rhythmic sense up from the earth into the body. You can use a partner to put some audible pure tones into a third person, the receiver. The two givers get close to the ears of the receiver, one on each side, and make a gentle embrace of sound. They restrain the amplification until the channel is coming in clear.

All creatures, all creation respond to sound. Plants and animals appreciate the simple notes of a simple handmade flute, for instance, as well as from our voices. Any one note can resonate rather indefinitely. If we practice attitudinal healing and centering our audible inputs will gladden the environment. When the tone and pitch sound good we are naturally inclined to expand the sound out in time and space. Maintaining the joy through a long breath multiplies the positive vibrations. We practice attitudinal healing with a song that opens the door for greater loving. The right song at the right time is a divine plan for the changing of persons. When a real acknowledgment is made and integrated - this permits us to move on to where it is better for us to be. Resonation is a vast tool for the integration of change. Picking the better pattern to embody, to follow; no longer is it hollow in these hallowed halls of lungs and heart, of throat and ears. They are full of *Godsong*.

Singing to Father-Mother God everyday is much better for you than listening to other people doing it. It only takes one sure sound to make a project work out right. A good blessing is hard to beat. There is really no better tool for any given job. No matter how difficult the road ahead may appear, it does always help to intone to Joy in the beginning.

Live Music Therapy/Audible Pure Tones is the remedy to use for all cases of negativity. Purer vibrations are brought forward in toning to replace the less pure ones causing the affliction. Basic toning treatments are structured around the resonation of a vowel sound. O expresses the Oneness of Creation. The Om is about wholeness. A expresses the divinity of matter, the power of the earth to bring forth life. A tones are low and deep. U expresses You, the Beloved, the Soul. U is good for compassion.

LMT/APT is for when you are bent out of shape emotionally and for when you are shining through. It works both ways: to transform negativity to positivity, and to further positivity. If you are happy it doesn't hurt to let out a shout of praise, or a whisper. Your positivity spreads out around you. The practice of the Good Sound furthers the Good Work. We might say all good work is the result of good sound. When we hear or read words that seem to indicate a wise way to go, we acknowledge, "that sounds right." To sound right an idea needs to be coherent. To sound right the chant needs to come from a place of communion. Being in a place of communion comes from the discipline and enjoyment of directing the drives of the body and emotions towards spiritual goals. When the attitude of the worker improves, workmanship is enhanced. Clearing an emotional obstruction is a kind of work.

When you really feel stressed and off center and you don't know why exactly, but you do know that the lower level of self is itching to make it worse - persevere with LMT/APT exercises. Isn't it interesting how chaotic energies lend themselves to the formation of beauty? Isn't it a relief not to hurt ourselves and not to hurt others when we feel parts of self uncontrollably tempted to do so? When we realize that destructive urges are part of our being and when we realize that these urges can be harnessed to advantage, we will no longer suffer because of them and no longer cause suffering to others. The magic of LMT/APT is how swiftly it repolarizes the emotions.

To accentuate our differences, to use the imagination to make a bigger picture of conflict than actually exists - isn't this thirst for alienation the real evil spirit within? With mentalizations of separation and feeling sorry for self, we are busy thwarting love's way. On one level we perceive the immaturity of it and on another level we just cannot keep from churning up some more bitterness and resentment. It is an historical addiction and the reason as much as anything for the endless chain of incarnations. The behavioral pattern serves to remind us how uncentered we are in the heart, how easily we slip out of grace and back into the muck. Certainly there's nothing wrong with mucking around. Unless, of course, we have something better to do with our time and energy.

Husbands express anger to wives. Wives express anger to husbands. Parents express anger to children and then children express it back. That which is objectionable is declared to be so important. Just so there can be rancor? Why? Why, because we are not expressing what we were married for - to love, to honor, to cherish, and we need to hear with our own ears just how off key we can get. It only takes one heartfelt word to dilate the whole problem. A tear is released because the duct in the eye opens, stimulated by emotion to its natural function of letting the moisture go. Modern man has his eyedrops but the built-in wash is still the best. It is so because it is more in the way of a whole bath. The physical eye is cleansed and the seeing process, as it is a connected awareness, is cleansed as well, and then all is well, because what is right in front of us is no longer obscured.

People use anger to get going just like they use caffeine. Hostility may not be pleasant, but it generally will push one through a mood of inertia. Of course, like caffeine, it leaves a toxic residue. Anger is a fuel, just not a very clean one. Too many people use negative forces to energize themselves which is why it is such a polluted atmosphere here, physically and psychically. There are clean alternatives to anger, caffeine, petroleum dependency. Solar energy is being used more and more. Balanced natural foods diet is being used more widely to keep the physical energy up without unhealthy stimulants. On the emotional level, joy is the stimulant of choice for those who wish to live more purely. Happiness translates into productivity just like solar energy translates into radiant heat. Basically, the dichotomy being observed here is that energy can be drawn from the earth or from the heavens. Joy is a heavenly potion. Anger is an earthbound drug. Solar comes from the sky. Petroleum fuels are pumped out of the earth and burned at no small cost to the environment. The main requirement towards moving into the solar age and the cleaning up of the atmosphere is insight. Insight of principle, design, and application is the leavening agent that will lift us into a higher vibration society. Using joy as emotional fuel requires the same things. Seeing by the gifts of heaven - insight and creativity, man learns how to run himself on the cleaner, more efficient, more productive energy. When we see people invoking hostility towards others to push themselves along, we can see how the anger is not actually based on the character or actions of the hostility object. Actually it is based on the need for emotional stimulation. When we see likes and dislikes, allegiances and betrayals, cascading after each other in a disturbing, irrational manner, we are seeing the need for periodic doses of adrenalin producing emotions. When people replace anger with joy as the mainstream of their emotional diet, they become gentler and more consistent, less neurotic and indecisive, more harmonious and agreeable to be around. Momentum coming mostly from joy versus momentum coming mostly from hostility is the difference between an integrated understanding of immortality and the lack of such. The miracle of life is a heavenly potential making an expression in the realm of matter. In terms of living our lives in the flesh, the more we adapt to heavenly sources of energy the better our lives will go here - more originality, more resourcefulness, more inspiration. The love of heavenly sources of energy is the love of freedom. The core of the anger syndrome is fear. The integrated understanding of immortality is the road out.

When there is a feeling of lack, a less than advantageous mindset is reversed by feelings of plenty. Joy means plenty of happiness. So we intone to joy in the beginning of the reversal process. The word joy said without conviction may not sound like much, but if you team up with honest emotional need and a willingness to activate, to resonate; then the three letter word can sound real big, and be a real swell from the ocean of life.

> "Joy to the world ... And heaven and nature sing ...
> Repeat, repeat the sounding joy."

People like to say that words cannot express ... it's beyond words. As much as words can't, words can. The ineffable does not have to be ineffective verbally. We can work within our consciousness to find a suitable way of bringing to mind a valuable theme. A song has words and music, and often the lyrics melodiously so presented, bring also to mind a picture. We can get the sound real centered so the melody, the words, and the picture will come alive.

The way of happiness does not interfere with the way of health. Those *body karma* patterns that degrade the health, which we rationalize we need for our happiness, is the area of self-deceit where the courage to change is needed for real non-fictional happiness to abide. Engaging in health degrading desires because we feel sorry for ourselves emotionally creates a vortex of negativity whereby the poisons of the emotions keep the body in a toxic, low-energy, confusion.

Feeling sorry for ourselves is the cause of all sickness and negative karma. What it takes to make contact with Spirit and keep up that contact, is to stop feeling sorry for ourselves. The more we feel sorry for ourselves, the more our lives will be a negative experience. The correlation is direct. Feeling sorry for yourself breeds dis/ease. Stopping it furthers health, wealth, and happiness. Self-forgiveness and forgiveness of others will follow when we extricate ourselves from the point of all hurting, which we know as the self-created syndrome of feeling sorry for self. The consciousness we use to replace the consciousness of lament is the consciousness of gratitude.

"Count your many blessings
Say them one by one
Count your many blessings
See what God has done."

If you are feeling sorry for yourself, no matter how infrequently, you need to stop. The point of your one-pointedness, your focusing power, must be the stopping of lament. Healing happens rapidly in the space of gratitude. Heartfelt gratitude is going only one direction and that direction is up. To stop feeling sorry for yourself is the contact point for self-transformation. The experience of the contact point is characterized by surrender. The persuasion and push of the ego are subdued and the higher communication invades directly.

If you can stop without LMT/APT, great. All I can say is LMT/APT is a terrific tool to give the emotions a positive place to go when it is time to leave the program of feeling sorry for yourself and time to integrate the program of feeling grateful for yourself. This is not a mental challenge primarily, although the mind sure can help. The contact point involves a change of heart. When the heart withdraws its energies from the syndrome of feeling sorry for self, no longer having the taste for that kind of emotionality, the nucleus of the addiction is then gone and the unfortunate obsession ends.

The more ways and the more often we can think and speak and sing about feeling gratitude for our lives, the stronger will be the consciousness toward making the change. A thought form, a sound form: these things are the builders of life. Consciousness is the space we make and are made by. We have impact on our environment and our environment has impact on us. This is why it takes some energy to turn things around. We need to build up some momentum going in the right direction only to reach the turning point. The more effectively we can *cop* to feeling sorry for ourselves, undermining the subtleties of the addiction, the more honesty and humility and grace will be going our way.

The negative, egoic vortex is strong. It takes much vigilance and determination to sway our *astral* momentum, our mood making, into the positive, bonding-to-Spirit, vortex. And more so to lock it in. The transformation happens when resolution heightens awareness to master the false formations of the egoic struggle to keep separate. We clean up our emotional act and thereby effectively embrace the truth of wholeness. Transformation means effective embrace.

Lip service is, of course, not transformation. But lip service in the way of heartfelt live music therapy can sure help you move through the reversal, whereby the anti-life sentiments are discarded. The details of your life - doing your diet right as you desire, social behavior, right, as you desire; all depend on keeping the contact point in good working order.

When it seems that as much as we know what is right, we still cannot master the integration of it, we need to check out the contact point. Will power is bodily distillation of spiritual connection. A person whose contact point is open and freely receiving the spiritual force is one who abides in a consciousness of gratitude. The consciousness of gratitude is busily recognizing the many blessings. It is the consciousness which is pulling in the Light and sending it in many directions. The consciousness of remorse and feeling sorry for self is, of course, busily trying to believe in misfortune. Because of this the contact point is not functioning properly and the input of spiritual force is diminished. The will power is not energized enough to follow through on the right course in regard to diet, social behavior, and other areas of concern when the will power is undernourished. To increase the resolution to effect positive changes, focus your attention to the contact point and keep cleaning out the emotional pollution until the channel is clear and flowing. If you get distracted, come on back. Spaced out? Try some deep chants and toning exercises. Stay grounded and distraction won't last.

We keep up the awareness and we keep up the determination. All it takes to reach nirvana is the heart commitment to do so. The commitment of the heart is, of course, not just lip and thought service, although lip and thought service in the way of affirmation of what is nirvana and what is not, is helpful. The commitment of the heart requires heart service. And a commitment is a commitment. It is not a make-believe commitment. Nirvana is based on reality, on real live continuous commitment. It is an interior process. It is not out in the South Pacific somewhere, necessarily, nor up in the mountains, necessarily, nor involved in any set of specific circumstances, necessarily. Necessarily, it is in the reflex of giving. The point of doing LMT/APT exercises, whereby we are giving the healing sound, is to keep the focus, not in mind, foremost, but foremost in heart, and in mind too. In this way, with perseverance, we stop feeling sorry for ourselves.

The more we hear from sung prayers of gratitude, the less likely outworn patterns of feeling sorry for ourselves will be of interest. People feel sorry for themselves because people get interested in it. You can unfetter your attention from this terribly unproductive syndrome by getting interested in something else, gratitude. Thank you so much for this life. Period. LMT/APT helps spread a consciousness of gratitude. No longer are we fraught with exceptions to the Rule. The gaps close. Human beings, with generous intervention invited to their Higher Selves, can be 100% operatives of Joy.

We have so much to be grateful for living in this time and space. There is a great redemption underway. Every man and woman is a potential alchemist by the simple virtue of being alive. Doing some kind of spiritual exercises helps keep the life processes in good tone, so the good seeds of cosmic orders may be planted in our hearts where they will grow into a better world. The athletic impulses from the soul delight in fending off the stagnant pools of lack.

Of course it is all right to get angry. It is a natural element on the way to joy. It is the character of anger to move through the emotions swiftly. When the movement is obstructed, there is, however, a perversion that begins and this is the cause of vocal aberrations. This is why our homes become permeated with unnecessary foul language and foul sounds. Anger was not sensed clearly, was not honored, and not expressed directly. Anger must move. If it sits, it pollutes. Family wellness is dependent on family members taking responsibility for negative emotions. Nothing, nothing, nothing, outweighs the priority of keeping this part of the home clean.

Procrastinating the release of negative emotions is the most pejorative procrastination there is. We will not enjoy mellifluous family life unless the *essential* home is kept clean. The way to ensure direct and due processing of negative emotions is to move into a mode and custom of sharing all the feelings that come up that may affect our attitude toward others. Lest we harbor and brood, we need to keep driving forward into the open waters of expanding love. If we do this from the beginning of the feeling, if we share the first signals, the sailing ship of the particular relationship will not flounder, but will absorb the message and be strengthened in its seaworthiness.

Communication, of course, is the key. The temple of wholesome family life is built by it. The beneficial communicatory practice consists of: 1) giving others a safe space in which to emote and speak by being able to hear what others have to say and to assist them in doing this by a supportive and tolerant attitude; 2) forthright and honest emotional expression, letting family members know as soon as we can where we are. In this way we can all be together no matter what is going on, because we have integrated a consciousness of unconditional love. Without this diligence, however, things come up we fear to speak of. We stuff the feelings, lest there be abandonment and strife. The truth is that we have already procrastinated too long in being emotionally honest and forthright. Further procrastination serves only to degrade the situation, driving us further apart. For the cause of your sanity and the family unity, push into the heart of the matter now. And this is how the how of doing it, is born.

There are things that make us a little nervous. For each of us these things may be different. For all of us the thing to remember is, that with a positive emotional state, things will go better in situations that challenge the nerves. If we have a bug about something or someone we need to *cop* to it, release it, and get clear again in the feelings; that is, be in a mood that is appropriate in emotionality to what it takes to be sane.

What any child needs is for his or her mom and dad to fall in love with Mother Nature and solve his and her own traumas, so she and he can help the child solve its trauma. Falling in love with Mother Nature is not just a lot of poetry. It is a basic level commitment. It is establishing a priority in one's heart. This commitment helps to heal the flaws in loving others and being loved by others that have imprisoned certain hurts from the past. When one's love for Creation sufficiently intensifies, negative patterns are de-energized, not just discussed. Discussing problems and ailments just reinforces an ailing problematic existence. To change we must search out the newer way so we can embody it. We must stop talking and take leave of our friends and begin to look for and be looked for; to begin, then, to see and hear.

What seems to me to be important to do is to spend a lot of time where you really enjoy the visuals. If you find you don't enjoy the things of nature, try removing your glasses or contacts if these things are used. See if you can get out of your head so you can see what is going on here in this natural setting. When we are excessively abstract and verbal we are in a fearful place. When we let go of this and come into a truly sensory moment, we will see the trees and things of nature again like when we were little children.

If we can no longer touch the space in us that experiences the paradise we are a part of, we will be separated from wholeness, from being *at-onement* with the wonder the child does feel (until the child too soon stops feeling it because the vibrations are not nurtured). The parent who has forgotten to keep touching that place where we are in love with Mother Nature gives to the child the dis/ease of not knowing everything is fine. What does our Mother say? The Beatles used these words, "Let It Be."

Kids get earaches because of too much mucous in the tubes and because of hurtful sounds. Moms and dads arguing harshly is a hurtful sound. The innocence of children will continue if we, as parents, can refrain from shaming them by a harshness that emotionally voids them out.

Parents should sing to their children. The higher vibrations need to be shared. Your infants, toddlers, and adolescents will greatly appreciate the special praise that is in the lovesong you give them. Maybe if we get enough emotionally-real praise when we are young, we will not be emotionally hampered by the unnatural syndrome of approval seeking behavior.

We can do everything better the next time around. This is the joy of parenting. Whatever was not perfect for you growing up, you can make this area better for your child(ren). Children can have healthier nourishment if we can take responsibility for making the gardens and being informed about what is really good for them and what is not. There can be less separation this time around. The ideals of family are realized by each of us sooner or later.

Many people experience dis/ease with social behavior based on "small talk" that is inherently nervous, lacking in real warmth, and that dissipates energy. "Small talk" is that speech which is emotionally irrelevant to the here and now of being together. When we understand the value of silent communion, we can introduce the social behavior modification process to others by saying something to the effect, "even though we have much that is productive to speak of, I am sure it is true we need most of all to nourish our emotional and nervous systems by just being together in silence."

Meditation on the breath is one way to control impure speech. If we are going to talk we have to breathe. If we pay attention to the breath we will pay attention to the speech. To say empowering words aloud is a form of LMT. If we will expend some energy truth speaking, we can soon be singspeaking, and from there it is just a continuous spreading of wingspan. We can take the time to get our energy together so the singing or sing-speaking will be heartfelt. "God bless you" is something we can say to someone with a lot of loving energy involved. It can be a real strong medicine LMT exercise.

We enhance the effectiveness of what we have to say by being more sparing, more totally centered, in what we say. Mind your own business and enjoy nature might be called the *numero uno* maxim of Zen. True solace may be experienced when capriciousness is put away. Simple offerings can be made.

There is no big reason to talk to each other for the sake of a social embrace. For the sake of a social embrace we can hug, work together, sing together, etc. Productive communication, verbally, that is shortened is more to the point. Right speech is that communication which serves to empower the truths of our loving natures. It is the needful dialogue used to further our abilities to help each other make the needful changes we each seek. Right speech deals with the realities challenging us to be more ourselves and less a personality mechanism that is going through the motions of being that which we are not, and that which, when confronted on a heart to heart level, we acknowledge to be of no value.

Healing song is an expansion of right speech into the realms of rhythm and melody and harmony. It is a way of getting the point across with more sensory input. Its effectiveness is due to the stimulation of the auditory dimension with pure tones that resonate and impact.

We need to be able to build up emotional energy in ways that are real. Sentimentality is always a little unreal. It does not get you where you need to go in making your approach to the Divine. We can congregate in ways that achieve pure cohesion. It can be real tangible and fills the hearts automatically. The physical body is used as a contribution to the experience of the heart. Nervously chatting is not it. Nor is moodiness. No contribution is made in either case to the formation of Love's celebration. What does it feel like to be a part of a larger organism than just yourself?

When people are overcome with emotion they generally try to suppress it, make it stop or go away. If we wish to use everything to our advantage, the attitude to choose in regard to emotionality is: yes, I am feeling some energy; where will it take me? When emotion comes do not be alarmed. Welcome it, for truly it is a divine nectar, a movement begun in Spirit now moving through you. Utilizing emotional energies creates great advantages. As much as the emotion may seem to be about people, places, or things; also try to keep your awareness of the bigger picture here with you as the emotion takes you for the beautiful ride it can give you when you let go. Expressing the emotion, we feel a measure of greater reality forthcoming, and this is what we learn: we can give it up. We can feel it lifting up to be released like *waves of the ocean of peace cometh. The ice man departs.* Be warm with the gift your emotion in its growing purity is trying to bestow to you.

Physical separation is no impairment, in essence, to the growth of loving in any relationship. Often a separation is a great gift. All reunions do occur that are needed by the loving hearts in question. Friendships can endure great vistas in time and space. The essential connectedness is one of the great blessings in learning to live the cosmic life. Being sad is not bad. It is a feeling that is real and as long as we don't let it steal our energy unto ineptitude, but work with it to build positive emotional attunements, it is a welcome guest in anyone's heart. Don't be too smart that you avoid being sad, because that's not really being smart. The pain is a gift. Just be smart enough when you have it, to use it to advantage. A song, a poem, a story, a picture - so many ways to get some beauty of the heart into a grounded form. We can express our emotions and move on to other things. We are blessed for having been close in a physical way, and now we are blessed in the way of being apart physically, but still close emotionally. The poem, the story, the picture, the song, etc., is a birthed being of your special feelings for someone.

Without grounding our emotions we not only can get sick by congestion of sadness (often heavy cold symptoms are experienced), but as a core health obstruction, we don't move on in our emotional relationship. All processes of the creative nature are this way. The poem written out is like the autumn leaf in its ripened beauty. We have to go round with the seasons of the heart or we will become depressed. So let's repeat. It is not bad to be sad. It is always a real gift in love's way. We just need to be intelligent enough about taking care of ourselves to use the emotions to advantage and not get suspended. Water flows on. If we need to cry we do so. This is usually how the change and unblocking begin. Tears assist in allowing self-forgiveness to grow. If we don't learn to allow our sadness to be, and use it, we will end up being mad, that is, using anger as emotional sustenance rather than joy. The use of joy requires ablutions and absolutions. Water and earth are the elements of fertility. The poem or whatever is the earth, the emotional context, the water. Let's be wise gardeners with our watery energy.

Over the years people can become attached to each other. We grow together. We can become separated. Intimacy changes. For happiness to continue we must find a way of transition. We can experience another level of bonding that allows us to preserve what we found so precious in the close family set up. The symbol, which in the physical, was always there for us, now needs to be brought forward in a no lesser, although subtler, dimension.

The joy of relationship boils down to working with the give and take as it is, not as we decide it should be. When we permit our relationships to be sacred, the secrets to functioning in them are not so hard to understand. When we opt for sacred, we opt for more determining factors to be present.

We can have what we need from any place or person whether we are there or with them, or not. We can move the essence of the place or person to us. We do this by moving certain emotional energies. Singing is a wonderful tool for doing just this. That mountain, that child, that lover, is with us where we are. We don't take a trip, they don't take a trip. We bring them to us, and staying at home, we keep the union strong. This is how we practice being in the center of the Universe, by keeping all relationships current in our consciousness.

I was living in Minnesota when I learned how loving a tree will set me free. Minnesota is still in some way the center of my universe. I now live in the middle of Texas and the trees and blue lake remind me of my former home. What I so much loved up there, I still love here. Clean, clear air; clean, clear water; midwest weather excitement; storms, waves, wind sounds; elms, oaks ... Because of the similarities it is very natural to feel like I am in two places at once. On an emotional level, I practice what might be called *psychic tai chi.* In this way I avoid feeling separated from any place that is dear and stay happily centered in the middle of my universe.

When separation occurs we feel a deep tug of emotionality in the middle of the body. Physically and emotionally we are disconnected from someone or some place we have been physically and emotionally connected with. Experiencing separation heightens the sensitivity to deep emotions and there is continuous need to let the sorrow express. The grief is real and so is the relief that fills in when the grief is released and expressed.

We can feel very alone living a married life, but in the context of being together physically, these feelings may not be so well defined. I believe there is a cosmic unity to emotional energy and that it is always present as day and night. Our life style choices set up patterns of buffering or diffusing this energy, or of making it more keen. To live alone may set up a more direct impact on self of certain primary emotional drives.

We are all here to get the clues on how we each will unify with that which we are emotionally charged to merge with. For the majority of us, merging primarily means mating with one special person. There are many of us also, who see something other than one person, or in addition to that, as the basis of merging-with and mating-to. We may see a place, a purpose, a change, a group, an alignment, or what have you, if called upon to define *where goeth* in us the emotional forces of unification.

Each person's life is their own little puzzle to work out. Relationships are the primary materials we work with in making our puzzle and finding how it will fit together so we can move along in love's way and wholeness progress. There is always a multitude of possibilities. We are tested to see clearly what we truly desire to energize. We come along after many lessons to a place of consciousness where we wish to be very carefully on target about the placement of our merging-with and mating-to energies. We seek a more effective and a more streamlined existence.

A lot of people are like chameleons, that is, they are good imitators. They take on whatever they are around. The blending, imitative quality can be to advantage or disadvantage depending on the company one keeps. Doing LMT/APT is good for the imitative tendencies and the independent ones. Developing your tone is a technique for empowering individuality. The specific ray of God that is you, that is, in essence, anchored as your tone, becomes stronger and more defined. By chanting the songs of union and healing contracted ego states, we enhance our openness to becoming more like that which we are drawn towards becoming. This serves the blending, imitative quality.

The first basis of human resource consulting is this: any quality manifested by any human is latent in any other human. "I would be so happy if I could be like..." You can be. The reality is this: the quality you desire for yourself is latent in yourself. What you need to do is bring it forward. Then you will be living amid the manifestation of the quality.

There is nothing that is impossible. Any statement beginning "I cannot" is inherently false. "I will not" is another matter. When people say to me "I can't sing," or whatever, I let them know that I don't believe that. "I don't want to sing," is more creditable, but still hard to believe. "I am afraid to sing," is very believable.

There are patterns of action that evolve to maturity, like building a home or learning the piano, that may seem like a complicated manifestation, but the whole rise of effort and accomplishment was derived from an every day basis of simple pursuits. The person who succeeds with her dreams and ambitions is most likely a person who is open to change. Becoming what one is not (yet) is relatively easy because of the latency phenomenon in humans. Whatever you see that you truly admire - how can you, in good conscience, not adopt it; make it you too? If you love yourself you naturally desire to embody it all.

The second basis of human resource consulting is this: do what you can do. Do not pine for what is not your experience (yet). Trust that where you are is where you need to be, and go on with it, so that where you are to be may come from what you are. If we stick to what we can do and begin to do it with some consistency, we will be moving along into clear areas of growth, following through with what we already know to be true. Backpedaling, hemming and hawing, all the ways of procrastinating, can cease and desist. We know we can do it. So at times when it seems we are not quite making it, let's not get lost in doubt. We do not want to be worrying that things may turn out awry in this matter we care so much about. Worrying does not help. Procrastinating does not help. Doing it, helps.

Worrying about the outcome of anything is not in our best interest. To worry is to have a consciousness of doubt and anxiety. Certainly it is more favorable emotionally and psychically to have a consciousness of peace and confidence, knowing that our needs will be met. The thing we can do to replace the pattern of worrying about things is to substitute affirmations. When the old pattern is starting to come forward again from its matrix of doubt and insecurity, we can immediately put our energy into a consciousness of peace and confidence by doing some affirmations. Doing affirmations means saying them or singing them in a heartfelt way.

The mundane logic here is that from a realistic point of view, we have no control over matters like finding a spouse or selling a home, and that in areas where we are dependent on factors beyond our personal control, we can logically acknowledge that worrying is not to our advantage and that saying our affirmations is. Whether or not we believe that saying or singing (!) affirmations is a magical success for-mula, we can comparatively sense that affirmations are certainly a better bet than worrying.

It's just fine to fantasize about the future, but if we are going to have that fantasy, if it is going to make it here physically, we need to accomplish the next practical steps in the logical progression of concrete reality. There is a definite tendency, when excessively caught up emotionally in the big picture of the changes we see coming, to neglect the tasks that will be needed to bridge together this time and that time. Right Now is the reality seminar we are in.

The mind tires and we return to the source of our lives where we can learn something we can put into words. But not until the perception comes without words will there be words to describe the precious something we learn that the return to the depths has provided. It can be said we work for a living and it can be said this way - that we make an effort to understand. Insight is deliverable to the one who is willing to meet God partway and who can do something for bringing that meeting together. The action of "figuring something out" is only a corollary action to the originating action that is honest speech to Spirit. We tell God what we need in many ways. It is not up to us to decide what kind of offering is acceptable. It is up to us to accept the kind of offering our experience reveals to be workable. Heartfelt toning, chanting, and singing are modes of offering that my life experience has always revealed to be workable.

When the sun isn't shining we have the opportunity to see if that Other Sun is shining. Rainy days bring the horizon in closer. Which means it is time to be feeling in oneself for the way and not just grabbing onto the sunshine. One's constitutional resourcefulness is always a reservoir no matter what the weather. Our religion is Joy and it's icons are perhaps easier seen in fair weather, but still we go on as before so that productivity continues day after day. We can't get to heaven if we don't try. We don't give up because we aren't there (yet), because we always have the option to try it some more.

Usually it takes a little while until the hearing clarifies and a little while until the music you wish to make clarifies. All of us are miniature outward conductors of the *wholer sound*. The *wholer sound* is the range of subtle bodies of resonance and pitch that can come into our sound making and into our experience of hearing.

We don't need to push new projects when understanding the aim is still young. Each project has a springtime and a harvest. When impatience is a problem we can take pleasure in the body itself. I can go swimming or water the garden, my thoughts are my own. I am not prey to them and they are not prey for me to chase until bewildered.

What can we say to the frenetic beast who is full of shoulds, the conversation in our minds that is not helpful? We can say, "what is needed here, patience or courage?" We can simplify the quandarying. Either way we go we are fleshing out virtue. Meaning truth is with us, meaning we do not have to take it from that unhelpful conversation which we know is unhelpful, because it pervades into the emotions an unsurety, a doubt, a grasping to know. There is no need to grasp the issue so hard. With a gentler hold, the course to be taken is revealed. No instance is going to pave the way. Patience and courage, day to day, will pave the way.

When wayward notions are coming through the mind, wait them out. This can be the forte of the spiritual overtone in the emotional center. When the centered notions, the truly on target and truly comforting brain waves occur, the emotional and physical processes can take up the movement so guided to be. Singing our song helps us to wait out the wayward notions.

If we can keep quiet about what is going through the mind, we can keep a wayward notion from causing trouble. When we share a still confused mentality with others, we are inviting trouble. If, in our hearts, we have learned that we really want something, it will come; and instead of rattling on about so many possible schemes for it happening, why not keep that basically pure thing between ourselves and our Maker?

Thoughts can make people unhappy until they learn to guide the mind to help make happiness along with the other members of the whole self. Excessive analysis is the kind of mentalizing that often illustrates the problems and struggles we create for ourselves. The attachment to the pains and sufferings, we call ours, and the resistance to giving them up has been very stubborn. Each of us has caused hurt to others and to self. We were doing the best we could as we were. It's just that we need to change. Then the hurting diminishes. As we change we clean up subtler and subtler areas of hurting self and others. I DO KNOW I AM CHANGING, these are powerful words. Being busy in and around the garden, befriending the life forms, is spiritual exercise. It is a very common grace, very easy to share.

Every day is full of therapies. As much light as there is in the sky - whether it is diffused and gentle on a cloudy day, or whether it is spontaneous and instantaneous like a shaft that momentarily displays the cast of the world in a much brighter angle when the rent in the clouds passes by the sun; there is the right feeling always about in the atmosphere to nurture consciousness.

I work at the simple needs of the environment. Each day I simply look about the land and see what can be improved. I do not labor for great durations. Generally I work at a pace that increases fondness. I rest and meditate frequently. The body exerts . . . the body pauses to enjoy itself in stillness. Sight takes pleasure from the meditative heart and the productive spirit, surveying the admixture of heaven and earth working out into its necessary beauty in this intersection, on this small plot. I do not dwell on what to do. I do not labor in abstraction. I do not have to sit in dilemma as over much thinking tends toward. I can get up and begin another stretch of simple chores.

Anything that can be formulated into thought will sooner or later need to be renounced. Certainly ideas can be useful, especially to keep our attention from lesser ideas. But it is always a matter of relativity - the head space, and not the center for functional integration. This is why a code of living that involves plenty of simple tasks emphasizing accord with nature is a preventative medicine for the duress of abstraction and the spirit-attenuating circumstances of self judgment.

To be overly concerned about stopping thought is to be frustrated by the quality of mind. Thought can be stopped but it will begin again. When "meditation" is only a temporizing of unhappy symptoms, and not the incubation of wholeness which is the cure; it seems to me, with a little courage and a little more patience, the soul's sweetness might be imparted more readily, more in the way of a sustainable continuum, in the direct way of life and the living. The cure for the disagreeable restlessness and relentlessness of mind is the improvement of the mind itself. The improvement of the mind is accomplished by the improvement of desire. This can be a very simple thing or we can make it very complicated. To desire contact with God is what trains the mind to cooperate and to assist in bringing forth the quiet that brings the sound, that brings the peace, that brings the understanding of what is vital and what is not. What I am saying is this - have a care lest you train yourself to struggle to meditate and forget that meditation, that is, loving God, the wish and the energy to do so, abounds. The beauty of nature reinforces this impetus for humans to do so. When the mind becomes natural it is not talking too much. It is talking just the right amount, because it is talking to the advantage of the whole self and not enamored of hearing itself beyond the level this part of self supplies.

There is a very direct way to use LMT/APT to cleanse ourselves of impure thoughts. We can allow the impure thought to express itself so we may know what we're up against. Are we being judgmental, defensive, aloof, envious, worrisome, derogatory, lustful, greedy, or what? We can save ourselves from being these things by eliminating the impure thoughts that cause and reinforce these things. We can eliminate the impure thoughts behind these unwanted qualities by selecting something to sing, and resonate inwardly, that highlights the antidote for the negative basis of the impure thought - the positive basis for purer thinking.

By singing something that embodies the healing thought form for an emotional imbalance, and especially through putting some real energy into the singing, we can begin to effectively de-energize the impure thought from our consciousness. If we have been resonating emotionally with the impure thought and similar thoughts for some time, it may take some time to clean this up and repeated LMT/APT exercises will be needed. Whenever the impure thought rises again in consciousness, it is time to repeat the exercise and resonate with the healing thought form which is building up a purer emotional basis. Many different songs can be used to treat the same area of imbalance. Or just use the same song; whichever you prefer.

Eventually we will be able to withstand any invasion of impure thought because the will has been made whole again. The self has the power to do this. With love and light, and empowering LMT/APT exercises, the self can become resistant to impure thoughts to a great degree. This requires a lot of loving vigilance and healthy emotional reflexes. Just like we train for physical coordination, we can train for emotional coordination. LMT/APT is a powerful tool for developing an emotional coordination which only accepts pure thought forms as seed energies of emotional force field empowerment. The LMT/APT technique for doing this is very straightforward. Simply select a song or part of a song to treat the impure thought form. When you sing, allow the meaning of the lyrics to saturate your consciousness. Repeat and be filled by your sounding with the joy of renewal and transformation.

The covets, the wraths, the irrelevancies, and so forth, are rebuffed by the positive-alignment-dynamic-tensioning of the *Spiritual Will Commandering Force* you are using to subdue the impure elements of self. We are all in tour of duty on the planet to undergo purification for:

Feeling sorry for ourselves
Filling ourselves with confusion, guilt, and denial
Being angry, being fearful
Wanting unneeded things, wanting to hurt others
Et cetera

We can dedicate a concentrated period of LMT/APT each day to strategically gain the upper hand on our "stuff." This is a very active mode of live music therapy.

1. Call forth all unbalanced feelings and impure thought forms.
2. Allow them to exist and express to you.
3. Refute them emotionally by on-key singing, that is, heartfelt singing.
4. Utilize lyrics which address the desired behavioral mode.
5. Repeat and acknowledge inwardly that the replacement mode is more attractive.

One at a time the impure thoughts and emotions will come forward, and one by one, by reverent song, this wholeness-diminishing "stuff" is de-energized further each day we practice our LMT/APT "torpedo" sessions. The process will work if you stick with it. We can completely succeed in our missions of work and happiness by clearing away any dominant impressions upon the will of impure thoughts. I strongly suggest you do them throughout the day as needed, whenever the impure thoughts, the "I.T.'s," do arise. They need not invade our consciousness any further. They need not intrude on our happiness. Don't let them waste your time. Sometimes you may need to earmark them for a later session with self. Cleaning up consciousness is just another job. If it gets done, it gets done. The sounding part of this technique gets the body involved. The will center is open to our ascended entry through the gates of boot camp purification training where we have trained ourselves to only serve the highest good/best interests of the heart.

We can sing songs and do the job of keeping the emotional house clean. The sounds of joy and determination really give an empowerment to self to get this purification fully integrated. In song there is fullness. Impure thoughts of lack are seen, in the Spirit of fullness, to be lies. The truth is fullness, not lack. The righteousness of song is what we use to keep the righteous plan in hand, to keep us on course with the source of all the things the plan needs to succeed. Songpower is manifestation power. Yes it is.

We can fill ourselves with impure thoughts when we feel how people who have been close to us have not united with us like we wanted them to. No matter what we may have done to alienate them, some of our emotions are not very interested in such logic. Our emotions can express feelings of alienation from people we expected to love us more. These emotions can dream up a lot of pictures about how we will make them pay for this alienation we feel. These pictures show them realizing how sorry they are that they forsook us. This kind of daydreaming can never slake the thirst for real love that emotions of alienation are badly needing.

Endless pictures of "love's" revenge can be created, but there is no real love to drink here; nothing real to heal the heart's anguish. The facts of the emotional pain we have caused others seem less conspicuous than the facts of our suffering. It is very difficult to get ourselves oriented to feeling their anguish. This is where the freedom is found. In compassion for their feelings of alienation, we are liberated from creating further pictures of alienation. It is sometimes a very tough drink to swallow - the hurt we have caused others. We need to be very strong to do it. LMT/APT can give us that strength to resist blaming others for our personal alienation and to resist all the impure thoughts that come from having done so.

The perpetrator in me of impure thoughts, negative emotions, erratic and crude behavior, and other unworthy "stuff" too numerous to mention, can easily be found and confronted. I just look in the mirror for a while and sing at him. I wish to be stern with parts of myself, so I administer some strokes via a song selection of charged lyrics that expose and chasten. While I am looking at myself and singing to myself, I also find the reflection in the mirror of the Good Me, the Christ-Self, the me I am passionate to become. That face is brighter, more kindly, and more in balance. Seeing the Good Me inspires soundmaking of another kind - affirming the Christ connection.

Watching the mouth as I sing is very interesting. With each word the position of the mouth changes. Here and there along the melody I notice the lips quiver. I see tears and smiles. I see all my different faces, and then just no-face, just brightness. These face to face live music therapy sessions are a real tour of the whole self.

Every person will have a different and unique collection of healing songs. I have filled several notebooks with songs from many sources. These notebooks are a great wellness and wholeness resource. The diverse collection seem to open every door imaginable. I have learned a song medicine for all the lacks and gaps in my consciousness that I have become aware of.

I choose songs to be in my notebooks according to word content and musical appeal. I need, firstly, to be in strong agreement with the verbal meaning of the song. Sometimes I am only interested in part of a song. Wherever and whenever I am exposed to a song that really lifts me, I want that music to become a part of my life. I make it so by writing it down and learning to sing it.

Greens, fish, tofu, sei-tan, falafel, to name a few, can satisfy the craving for meat. When we have removed once the craving from its object we have begun to study the craving itself. We may find other substances that can nicely do as the object of the craving. We are free to transfer our affections to other foods (or other sensations). Maybe we can get from donuts to dates, or from steak to beans (or from anger to joy). Maybe we can get there with the basic nature of the craving still intact. We can create a path of purification without divorcing the lower self and discover that it has the same desire to lighten up if given a chance to try some new combinations. The point is that it is a bit much to foist abstractions on the body, what with the emotions hurtling allegiance to and fro. The mind has the right idea of course, but what is the mind going to do about it? Perhaps to begin, to attune to the whole self with an attitude of care and ingenuity. We can suspend judgment and nurture the transitional nature. When the emotions are not alienated, the body will not recoil. Progress is made because we don't get uptight about being right. The idea is right; yes, we can say it again. And it's just the pinpoint start. A revolution needs to revolve. Consciousness can move around the location of change. It can scout. It can be useful, rather than stuck. Change is accompanied by happiness. Unhappiness is caused by insulting the integrity of the whole being. Learn how to avoid causing yourself unhappiness and you learn how to avoid causing it to others. Be kind to animals, yourself included.

Good nutritional practices can be furthered by applied live music therapy. Doing LMT/APT's before a meal probably will improve the taste of the food besides improving our attitude about eating it. It is not physiologically helpful to eat when we are upset. If we feed ourselves psychologically first, a good meal will follow when it needs to. Often people will eat when they are not hungry - from patterns of the time of day, or being bored, or lonely, or ungrounded, and it is a poor nutritional program even if we are eating the right foods. We maybe need to hug someone or sing a line of a simple song to get over the poor programming. If we want to be at our best we need to make the positive efforts that assist the positive programming. Before men and women can stand up and arise to their vision of life purpose, they need to be able to sit down and chew their food properly. Our job is to love God, and by asking for it and affirming it, we get around to doing it.

When we experience regressions in evolving diet and so forth we learn what we're up against in making a change in consciousness be permanent. Our goal becomes, through the repeated pains of regressive behavior patterns, to keep the torch of the new consciousness, the preferred consciousness, lit and operational, no matter what circumstances we may find ourselves in. It takes some work to change consciousness in areas of health and it takes more work to maintain the change. When we experience regression it means that we have more work to do in maintaining the change. The old pattern slides back in from time to time. Perhaps certain circumstances stimulate the regression and there is a clue to establishing more control. With greater vigilance we can come to keep it together in any circumstances. The key is vigilance. We won't go backwards if we watch where we are going. We tend to lose our vigilance when we enter into moods that are imbued with an association to the past and the unevolved habits thereof.

We remove addictions by removing the nature of addictiveness. The nature of addictiveness is a misqualification of the nature of obedience, which is an essential theme in our evolution. Not wishing to pervert the divinity of our nature, we pledge our obedience to the highest good and withdraw our attention from that which is not.

If we don't feel beautiful we can take a hike. A little rapture over Mother Nature goes a long way in the project of self-beautification. When we are sick, fatigued, depressed...we can take ourselves to a quiet place. We can look at the cloud or tree or whatever and just breathe. For the fun of looking forward to a new day we can be up and awake for the dawn. We can hear the wind's first song of the day, see the sun's first rays, and have the first good bits of *harth*. During the rest of the day we can be barefoot as much as possible, without any clothes (if possible) for at least a short while, and we can take some time and effort to minimize the dependence on any crutch.

Cleanliness is next to Godliness and the best place to start to clean the house is to scientifically purify the diet. We need to understand what our organs are for with an intimate knowledge, not just a passing interest in the concept of them. When our home or office is untidy it is an obstruction to our awareness of the grace of the space. When the body is untidy - same thing. Just like impure and too heavy a diet makes us feel less than our best, so also do impure emotions and thoughts. When we lighten and purify the diet we feel lifted up. When we do our LMT/APT exercises there is an anti-gravity movement sweeping away denser bits of consciousness.

LMT/APT exercises build up juice in us like a plant stores up the radiance it is given for new blooms. When we do our toning attunements regularly, we lower the amount of time we spend in the various deliriums of negativity that out-of-balance moods tend towards with associated confusion and ill ease. When live music therapy is readily supplied for the family, positive emotional reflexes are developed by everyone.

If you are not singing, and inside, a little deeper than the fearful mentalizations of inadequacy and rejection, you know you want to be, you can console yourself with this: "like other things in my life that I have experienced frustration with that were important to me, I know if I keep pushing, in singing also, the ability will eventually be born." When we creatively push to overcome obstacles in ourselves, we touch back to the time when our feelings were hurt. The shame that has not been cleared, the hurt that has been suspended, has since then, crimped the flow of expressive energies based on the potentialities of the whole system. Vocal expression is one area of social encounter where stored traumatic embarrassment really hinders the flow of natural abilities. Any "can't" in the consciousness is a crimp in the full legioning of bodily-emotional impulses. The contracted pains and blocks from earlier experiences are released as the nervous system is restored through actions of forgiveness and renewal.

If you are wondering if you are ready to sing, ask yourself how grounded you are and ask yourself to honestly confront the emotional contents. Then you can say to yourself, "this is what I am really feeling and this is what I want to sing." You choose the words to fit where you are coming from emotionally. If you are not sure if you are all that grounded, you can get some exercise; maybe there is some homestead chore or a child to nurture.

Let's take for example, the emotionality of "I am a little anxious about the future." We do not have to be in a tizzy to have emotional content. We can just be in the steady stream of persevering in what is right for us to do, the challenging nature of which is always a basis of emotional energies. We have reason to sing and resonate the truths we seek to follow, for we are human and subject to self-doubt and self-confusion and innumerable vexations. The live music therapy we create for ourselves is a nourishing meal as we continue to stay centered. We sing to compassion and we sing to courage and patience and so forth, to keep positioning ourselves advantageously toward overcoming our personal limitations. Overcoming personal limitations is the path we take in discovering and clarifying and following through in that which is for the highest good.

People tend to be anxious about money, mates, family relations and relations with friends; about work and matters of conscience, about health . . . This stress can be productive. Live music therapy is our best plan for converting all the dross to gold, because live music therapy is, in essence, a process of conversion. Experiential advances in wholeness and cosmic trust convert us to being more of who we really are.

One way of slowing down and tuning into a chant, is to count the words on your fingers by lifting up one finger per word (or syllable) from your fist as you chant. For example: 1-THE 2-LORD 3-IS 4-MY 5-SHEPHERD 6-I 7-SHALL 8-NOT 9-WANT. Most chants have a very countable number of words. The toning exercise is what counts and counting the words can further your interest in making the time dedicated to chanting count for something in terms of healing and balancing and energizing. Make each part of the meaning count for strengthening by words. Make the sounding of each word count for strengthening by sound. Chanting is a repetitive expression. You can plan to do a certain minimum number of repetitions or until a certain level of energy is reached.

The benefit to consciousness of live music therapy may be realized without making outward sound, without physically singing. The song can be heard inwardly. It is played by memory on the *inner radio.*

Whether physically sung or not, it is the treatment to consciousness the song provides which restores balance. The process of understanding ourselves is not dependent on making outward sounds. Auditory stimulation, whether by an inward or outward hearing, energizes the process of understanding, and the value of singing to emotional health cannot be overstated.

Another LMT/APT technique is the "consciousness game" format. The orientation is playful. For example, we might explore what songs we can think of to sing for each of the seven deadly sins. One by one, we focus on each of the seven "deadlies" and find something to sing which really fits into what we feel it takes to avoid slipping in that area. No matter from where we enter - be it in the midst of serious emotional experience, or just in a playful, mental mode; if the singing is heartfelt and the sounding empowerment is active, we will be benefited. "Consciousness game" approaches to LMT/APT fit into relaxed times of companionship. We might play with the signs of the zodiac or the elements of nature as game formats. The game simply amounts to finding songs for a list of descriptive words. The purpose of the game is to exercise our singing powers and further affirm desired modes of consciousness. The fun is in brainstorming for songs that fit each topic.

Interview yourself. Does LMT/APT work? Have you done your alleluias today in one form or another? Some way, any way, of releasing the negativity that binds you from being of excellence? Alleluia is a magic word. However it is spelled, it is beautiful to say and to mean. And sung, then the marvel begins to be sown.

All we need to be live music therapists is to be able to:

1. Do our tones lovingly. Give the prayer offering of the Sound within outwardly.
2. Hear the sounds of nature and help others to relax and listen in.
3. Know some chants and songs to sing at the right time.

LMT/APT can stimulate the action of release and it can be the action of release. We sing the truths, we hear the inner sound, and we speak out spontaneously from a more resourceful consciousness, so that our inner being word on the matter can externalize to present the understanding needed to move any situation into balance. All we have to do is get the words of the meaning we wish to *cop* to, sung or sung-spoken three times.

Words can be sung or sung-spoken with any length pauses whatsoever and whenever, in the singing or sing-speaking of the resonating prayer exercises of LMT. The pauses are used to breathe and meditate on the sound and the meaning. If we feel a little locked up vocally, doing our audible exercises quietly and gently, and using the pauses, will give us a helpful mood of modesty and diligence. We can push through the door in other ways. Going to a hot springs where one's hearing can be filled with the thundering roar of geothermal energy, locked up sounding powers may, by the stimulation of Nature's sound and osmosis with it, break free. In this way we get in touch with a deeper sound and more volume by entering a place of deep sound and potentizing volume. The power of the earth is utilized to help individual expression come forward. The physical sound in you is of the earth as well as it is of heaven; and as it is nurtured by heaven, it is also nurtured by the earth. Waves crashing on the shore, waterfalls, thundering storms, rustling foliage, are other examples of natural sound that can be utilized.

In all blockages of expressive energies, vocal or otherwise, ask yourself what might be missing consciousness-wise; what imperfect attitude is being held and is holding the full complement of juice from flowing? Why are you withholding the greater measure of empowerment?

A breaking through vocal blocks healing prayer might go like this:

> Heavenly Father, I am open to be of service. Please help me to go through whatever I need to go through to become Your Instrument. Earthly Mother, I am open to be filled with the sounds of nature. Help me be of service in balancing the negativity around the planet and in myself.

If you need to use a tape or a record player like a ballerina learns with a barre, that's fine. Just make sure you do your part so you can grow by doing your sounding exercises. When a sweet note comes along on the record or tape let your tone out and hum along. There will be certain notes that certain words belong to in the song that are favorable to you for emotional and musical resonation practice.

If you are trying to help someone open their throat, you might find it helpful to massage the shoulders, the belly, the chest, and even the throat in a gentle way; or by lifting the vertebrae to a more erect posture. You can encourage the person to increase their oxygen intake. Mostly, just resonating something audible that is simple and easy and natural for them to join will get their sound going.

Intenser methods are sometimes appropriate. On one occasion I walked with someone out into a lake. Beautiful fall colors surrounded the body of water known as Medicine Lake. I led her out to where the very cold water was up to her shoulders. It was sunny and fairly calm so her ears and throat stayed warm. The cold shock to the rest of the body, along with the beautiful scenery, opened up her voice.

The thing that often eludes us in walking is the sensibility of effort. We take the accomplishment of our native stride for granted. But do we take for granted the quality of the time spent? Often, I think not. Slippery places along a shore or steepnesses with sliding scree accost us quickly to see we must pay attention. But much walking is done on dry level ground where we may be tempted in our abstract parts only to regard the span of our walking, our thoughts, and the scenery. Walking, or singing, simple as it may seem, or easy, is given to be on behalf of the whole universe. The energy of the body is provided by the energy of the sun. We know the story and we can remember it in whatever we do, and all that we do will be enjoyed to the max.
We appreciate every little thing. All the components of making it happen are to be relished. The person who wishes to play a musical instrument can make each playing, each level, a symphony unto itself. Psychological composure allows the body to render a wonderful performance of the most elementary things. We can be hearing something good right from the start. When the inner life is making the mark, the mark will be obtained outwardly as well. To be motiveless is to be free from psychological processes that retard. The expectation of gratification does not make gratification. Gratification comes in its own way because Time makes it so when we are motiveless. Each moment is precious is a cosmic fact. This is why Time makes the experience wonderful for you as you are willing to change yourself so the new and improving you can keep coming through. Locking yourself out from the wonder means not that you have made a

blunder, but that you are holding yourself to creating some effect and consequently the desired effect is not being made. You are simply forgetting your part in the cooperative process of manifestation. You are trying to bend Creation to your mind's will, instead of using your mind and will towards the advantage of your body and soul. The state of being we enjoy the most is the flowing, giving, and receiving process, in which learning is a continuous unfoldment to the senses.

A live music therapist practices emotional healing as a personal duty through self forgiveness and forgiveness to others. A live music therapist works on herself towards wholeness and practices ways to provide the right music at the right time. Live music therapy is shared with someone for the purpose of emotional healing and strengthening. The right music at the right time is that music which cleanses when release is needed, that music which strengthens when strengthening is needed, and that music which calms when calming is needed. When we can see what we have been holding onto, the song has done its job. Good energy is free flowing again. The bend in the back, the sour grapes, disappear. Something has taken its place. The appearance of Joy. Joy shows Her face when there is mending. By empathizing with someone we can feel what song or piece fits and play it when the patient is patient enough to tune in. The first job of the live music therapist is to make sure the patient is hearing. When the patient hears, amends can be made and the patient, then, is no longer a patient. The person becomes clear and active; no longer reactive, confused, and sluggish.

The way an LMT worker might work with the use of taped music that would still be live music therapy, would be to use the recording to help promote the student's toning and singing exercises. When selecting a musical piece for a patient to hear and receive, this should be done without the tape recorder. Treatment of LMT should be live. Healing transmissions are totally alive.

The work of live music therapy is in some ways like the work of psychiatry. Before the musical treatment is provided some kind of diagnosis is required. Some live music therapists may be able to obtain the necessary information on the emotional condition they will musically treat from a strictly intuitive basis. The standard, basic level, technique for obtaining appropriate data on the emotional condition is the common psychiatric approach; that is, listening to the patient discuss her emotional situation.

A tape recorder can be utilized as an aid to the diagnostic process. Both patient and therapist can listen to the patient's discussion as many times as necessary to discover the key emotional points on which to base a live music therapy treatment. This may be especially helpful in tracking through discussions concerning relationships and the suspended resolution of buried emotional experiences.

It is important to understand that live music therapy can be utilized by the individual alone as self-therapy, as well as in the common style of client and therapist. In self-therapy the individual can study tape recorded discussions of talking to oneself. Studying written journals is also a basis for diagnosis. In any case, whether as self-therapy, patient-therapist style, or even in group format, the key process is to interpret data concerning emotional conditions in need of healing.

The story of every unhappy experience and relationship has certain key themes. In understanding these themes we will be able to diagnose the specific block of consciousness and formulate desirable treatments. Then the singing can begin. Where blocks of consciousness have commonly existed for some time, it is generally desirable to apply the song or songs formulated in a healing session for some time after the session, in a regularly scheduled way.

A discipline of live music therapy for the curative benefit to emotional patterns which have caused past unhappiness will be the best preventative approach for avoiding future experiences of like nature and for generally strengthening the emotional constitution in that area. Regressions in emotional behavior, as in diet and other areas, can be prevented by a conscious choice to sustain the upliftment received in a systematically vigilant and grounded way. LMT/APT can be a systematically vigilant and grounded way to sustain desired changes and overcome regressive tendencies. Whether this process of evolution, or any other, delivers desired results is, of course, always dependent on the integrity of each individual's application.

The standard diagnostic approach for live music therapy can be summarized in three stages:

1. Presentation through discussion, monologue, written journals, or however, of pertinent data to emotional conditions.

2. Interpretation of data and distillation of key themes.

3. Based on discovery of key themes pertaining to the blockages of consciousness, specific chants or songs are selected for treatment.

All good things in life evolve from the effort to place learning in a nurturing regard. Something learned and expressed is a gain. The goof-up of attitude is transmuted by the loving understanding that comes from the motivation to keep growing and healing and progressing in the development of a more hospitable, life-giving, consciousness. These sessions we have where we pull back to center and can ground in written words, pictures, or however, the psychological atmosphere of what it will take to improve - these sessions are the food of self understanding. Taking in the clues that experience brings of what love and peace are not, and what therefore can be deleted from the mood menu, we can increase our skill in operating the selector lever of self-expression, weeding out unproductive choices. It is not so much of a tree for a person to have enough paper for a self study, a self-building project.

Improvisational lyrics and sounds come into an enthusiastic practice of LMT/APT. Improvisation adds a dimension of creativity to the positive energy formation process. Creative expression does not have to consist of an improvisational, extemporaneous structure. Any song known to millions, and sung millions of times, is creatively expressed when it is creatively felt, that is, when it has heartfelt content. And certainly any kind of improvisational energy within a heartfelt context is always welcome. Improvisational energy can enter expression lyrically, melodically, rhythmically. The live music therapist basically works within an improvisational orientation in bringing together musical treatments. Whether she makes up a song on the spot or uses an oldie-but-goodie, what counts is whether it works for the patient. This amounts to much the same kind of thing food preparers get into who have the knack for putting odds and ends together to make delicious meals. People who have strong emotional motivations to nurture are naturally inclined to an improvisational tempo.

> You can compose many songs or just a
>   few,
> The quality will always remain in the heart
>   of creation.
> That's where nice sound is found.
> It is not found in originality necessarily,
> Nor in repetition necessarily;
> Neither does a six piece ensemble,
> Nor does a whole orchestra guarantee.
> The birds know why.

The way a pitch is sounded is a variable always worth respecting, the maturation of singing in any song. What the ear is needing to hear and what the voice is needing to express is released in a flowering, even if it is only for a second. The moment happens when beauty and truth can be externalized vocally for the rapture of yourself and perhaps some others. Maybe it can come through on tapes. Certainly the spiritual orientation of the composers and musicians can be gleaned. But I think it's important to realize we are going to need to make our own music for wholeness to succeed. My favorite original song involves only one guitar chord. The fingers of one hand never move; they stay in place. But the variations on the melody and rhythm possible are really rather infinite.

You can let go of that sound you like to make at the strangest of times. Perhaps in an almost unnoticed moment the energy breaks through. An efficient way to channel energy is through the voice; whatever you are doing - making friends, building a house, feeding folks, raising kids, singing a song. The simplest way for most of us to let go of this instrument is to begin with a tone that we believe can make contact for us. We become open to the energies Spirit can impart. It is always a matter of contribution to the common cause that lights up the message. The love center in the human must be fed those things that vitalize it if the life force in the individual is to increase.

In the last analysis, trying to cope is never the ultimate dope. The ultimate dope is to give it up. The fact is, if people were not attached to their dis/ease they would not be suffering. If people can truly give it up, they can be free of dis/ease. That means breaking all attachment to it. An effective prayer is one that helps to produce a good outcome. What greater gift is there than health? This is why God will take your suffering and exchange it for freedom from the bondage of infirmity. When you really see that it serves no purpose, you will, in your heart, really mean business and the so-called miraculous remission can happen. But you, wise believer, know that it is no happenstance. You know what kind of loving mercy has been involved. Because in yourself, and you are the extension of God - the One who can give health, you have come to the point of no return. Because in terms of bringing real comfort to yourself you have dropped the notion of feeling sorry for yourself, which is the crux of the problem of attachment to dis/ease. By dropping the attachment there is no longer any problem. It has cleared up, vanished, and certainly all your physical health methods have helped build up your determination to get free of the karmic obstacle; but in the ultimate sense, you crossed over by the grace of God and by your effective surrender.

We all love the glimpses of the fuller dimensions. Life is more of a unity in those moments. The person who works to develop this receptivity is a mystic. The mystic is "addicted" to seeing God everywhere. Concentrating our visual energies to intently focus on something, or on nothing - but to hold focus, can very definitely energize the sounding process.

We thank Spirit for the way that has led us here and for providing the rain and materials by which this lawn may grow for beloved souls to gather and, in their ease, take the communion the glade shares. There is nothing to beware of in this park. All is gentle to the body and eye. We can look towards the filtered sunlight and relax any nervous stress in our eyes. We can close off thought and relax any stress in the emotions. For here we are praying together without effort, eyes open to the light of the world. What is meditation? It is that which is naturally present. We don't need to close our eyes for it. It is revealed in the earth as it is in heaven. "God is everywhere." If we must be verbal, let's say this. When we keep busy loving everyone and everything without exception, the Dispensation will flow. Heartsong will fix the lapses.

When the ear and voice are open to God's love, truth is audible. It is the Word in its non-verbal dimension that purifies the verbal consciousness. In the last analysis, analysis will bring you no closer to where you need to be. It is contribution that closes the gap. Contribution is a vibrational exchange. All the words we speak in one lifetime, all the talk (I heard a Harvard science professor claim), will not heat one cup of tea. But one note sung with conviction can shatter glass. What I am saying is that the nature of sound is the nature of impact. Knowledge without love is useless information. The dis-ease must be dealt with, not just diagnosed. When energy is supplied conditions can change.

We can let the *soundmaker* deep inside of us be uncaged. The contribution is love. It is released in each of us by giving. What really have we got, what really do we own, but this moment here and now? Let's make it nice, because thinking it is somewhere else is really to be very poor indeed. So let's seize the moment, each of us, and let the wealth of love shine in.

Spirit has a great musical army that invades the realms of negativity and defeats the enemy. Heaven is in motion. The wind and waves provide helpful symbols. If we are going to be holy, we are going to be whole. When we sing and it sounds holy, our perception of wholeness is extended. All of us need to make some music for wellness. It is a panic sometimes to make a start because we are so sensitive. It may seem like raising the dead to get your throat open, but we look around and see that everyone is going to make it into the Choir.

If there is energy coming in the intonation it will naturally resonate and the balm of vibration will begin. Like a dawn the toning power comes to life. The singing begins quietly, thoughtfully. The voice of the personal ego drops further back and the voice of Spirit comes further forward in the joyous paradise of connecting live sound with cosmic current.

By letting loose our loving vibration we are letting the creation around us know we care. What we learn from live music therapy is how interrelated this existence we are playing in is. In order to play our parts well, to have balance and stamina and adaptability, we need to get the Virtues working in us and for us and with us. We do this by offering contributions in other ways, but probably most importantly in respect to physical manifestation, through sound and invocation and resonation; that is, by sounding off for some purpose that is declared by verbal meaning or symbolic meaning, and by getting into the music of it for the joy and well-being of so doing. Hymn is tune and hymn is vow.

What wonderful things we can hear come through the throat and heart of the egoless state of paradisiacal childlike innocence. The point is not to evaluate the sounds we are making aesthetically or however we may presume to evaluate expression or understand it. The point is to experience what making sound is useful for. How am I to energize myself? That is what is relevant mentally. We can understand how the experience we have created for ourselves does energize us.

Staying in the wonderment and staying out of the ego controls is the correct position to be in to participate in the sacrament of beautiful music. We can feel so purely, and so *unattachedly* so, the angelic transmission of sound. We can be the instruments for the release of divine music. The positioning for so doing is, essentially, an ego-shedding process. There is nothing that needs to be done with this experience. If we try to capture it, to harness it, it will no longer be our experience.

We can choose to handle these holy transmissions from the perspective of the ego's eventual intrusion, as strictly a gift. Our joy in those minutes was incredibly real. Whatever the gift of melody and lyrics was, is what it was; and we can let go of the futile instinct to try to reconstruct what we experienced because what is really prized is the essential knowledge that what can be today can also be tomorrow. The vitalizing vibrations that entered our bodies in the experience of receiving the heavenly music can enter again. Something about movement, I'd say, has been part of my personal physical plane focus when it happens. What I become most aware of in myself is the empowerment of Heart shifting forward into Overdrive. It is a blessing, a time of peak learning and self-understanding.

When the Current moves them, humans can practice the arts of having no pretense before God. By letting the spiritual force invade their bodies and emotions, the throats and hearts are captured and much beauty results. To be like God, we have to practice what God does.

Singing is an exercise mostly of the heart. To have a therapeutically productive musical expression, all we need is a sense of *at-onement.* When we sing therapeutically we are being very *un-phoney.* We are being present, and in being present, being true to the cosmic vision indwelling. There is nothing to beware of in opening our heart to someone. If we can open our hearts we can sing. We can let the voice loose. This is how we give what we have to give. And Spirit will add the rest.

When the transition transpires from singing by ourselves to singing with others we feel a lot better than we felt before. Singing by ourselves we were expressing emotion, but not sharing it. Now we are sharing and often we learn that we don't need to rehearse. When we sing that will be rehearsal enough. The right emotion is the truth and the application of it is the clarity. The song is clear when the singer experiences truth.

God has given us a voice, a way of translating the energies that flow from the consciousness of love. Music is an art of confrontation. We are bringing our music to the ears of others to communicate to them, to address certain issues between us. We have, as power-to-vocalize, the emotion that we feel about these issues and these people.

Live Music Therapy might also be the name of a musical performing group that could be brought together and to good performing quality without a lot of structured practice. That is because live music therapy is based not on the demands of the ego, but on doing spiritual exercises and, by this virtue, able to utilize any person who wishes to be whole. Surrender is all you can say to yourself to find your participation.

Every neighborhood needs a grass roots LMT group. A LMT musical production team can be brought together by organizing a class in LMT and the creative processes of people sharing will then take over. It will be seen that attaining levelships of quality musical production follows rather effortlessly as a derivative of attending to business - namely, the healing work of live music therapy/audible pure tones. We let go of self-consciousness and bring in self-awareness. Concentrating on enunciation we acknowledge the verbal meaning. In this way truth speaks first and melody second. We want the sound to be beautiful because we want the therapeutic, educational service to be made.

One of the advantages of practicing sound yoga and music therapy is to have a release mechanism for creative energies that overbuild. When the voice (rather than sexual expression) is used to channel out emotional and sensual forces, this is something that can be spread to more than one lover. In effect, you can make love to everyone and everything. And this is done. Making music is right here and now like sexual love making is (or should be, anyway). It is simply a way to heal and grow by filling the atmosphere with audibly uplifting vibrations. It cannot be emphasized enough how helpful this can be.

Sensuality does not have to degrade. Sensual energies can lend their wisdom too. The problems we encounter because of sensuality all derive from the fact that it is very easy to get out of balance in sensual pursuits. Indeed, it is the pursuing of sensual experience that is often the cause of our errors. We can encounter everything as a contribution to wholeness and not be sidetracked - that is, come to feel tainted and impure, as long as we approach everything as an opportunity to expand our horizons.

Where sexuality has become empty, it is because it has become devoid of emotional contribution. The body can do the function; the mind can direct it to happen; but if there is no heartfelt context to the physical proceedings, all we have is proceedings. Each stage of intimacy needs to be enjoyed, needs to be an end in itself. We can realize a nourishing emotional closeness at any stage of specific contact and the uniting urge can be satisfied without further physical ado. People often concentrate too much on the genitals. These things connect in a timely and appropriate enough manner that really cranks the Spirit high. *Keeping the glow moving* means sharing high energy and intimacy in other ways, such as musical expression.

Putting our heads together can be a very high, intimate experience. We can put our heads together, temple to temple, and enjoy the peacefulness inherent in the process of minds becoming close. The stress of argument, excessive abstraction, and verbalization can recede as we close our eyes and meditate together. It is a gentle hook-up, and because of the gentleness, it is nurturing.

Contrary to what we generally hear and see in this world, the way of true romance is through purification. It is the love for Mother Nature and

Father Heaven that produces a happy trail in love's way. When the movement of consciousness is locking into Divine Assistance, success in human relationships is possible. Romantic relationships require more assistance than other kinds. We are each unique individuals and therefore different, but when it comes to bonding we need to come on to that joyous level where we are one, and thus the same, and be able to stick on that level. Here we discover how the awkwardness of being in separate bodies and egos is transformed and the kind of loving we have needed is shared. The way we need to go is much the same in many respects although we live in separate bodies, and the work of integrating the better patterns of diet, exercise, and expression is what fellowship can support. Although we may feel we have a special relationship with someone, unless we can also be unto each other in the universal manner of what every person will give unto every other, the special love will not be realized. This is the purification of attitude that paves love's way. It is characterized by humility and remembrance of the common goal. What is cleansed is the presumption of familiarity, which is cloying and takes the fine edge off our love.

It is not essential to be with someone. It is essential to love everyone. No greater love has anyone than the love for everyone. For where there is rancor - even towards one, the *astral plane* is a wobbly spaceship and our orbits are not as true as they might be. The blessings of guidance do not come to the one who has repressed love for anyone. Blocked emotions also block cosmic attunements.

An insult is just as good as a compliment. Maybe better. "You can't hurt my feelings" means all examination of character that rings true to me is to my advantage. If it is not true, it will not ring true, and what is not true has no power. What is said about me can only help my feelings because I use everything to advantage. Especially useful is the feedback from others, no matter how grossly presented, that assists me to focus on further refinement of self.

Sometimes we need to hug an enemy or ward off a friend. As we need to maintain our individual balances, we need to compensate for the off-balances of other people who enter our space or when we enter into theirs. A quick decisive hug to an emotionally off balance person who tends toward antagonism and hostility may be an effective restraint. Sometimes a very congenially surfaced person has some ulterior motives that need to be resisted openly, lest the conviction gain in them that they can perpetrate something.

It is part of being human to be contrary. There are times when being contrary may be to advantage. Jesus got contrary with the money changers. He saw the exploitation the culture was permitting and He confronted it. Jesus pioneered in this area and many others have seen when it was right to be contrary. Most of us, however, still space this out. We do not object when the time is at hand to do so and, consequently, we find ourselves being contrary when it is time to be receptive. If we are contrary when it is time to do that, we will be receptive when it is time for that.

When the volition is not applied and the subconscious accumulates guilt and frustration, we will be struggling against ourselves. We will be repressing the Yes we need to make. Going back to the subject of toning and live music therapy as spiritual exercises, it is important to understand that we may feel strong resistance because of what is coming up from the subconscious. It is thereby important to understand the necessity of struggling beyond feelings of debility, obstacle, and conflict, into the feelings that breakthrough provides. When resistance is resisted, contribution is made.

We cannot be poised and be complacent. Balance does not keep that long. Effort must be continuously supplied, like a river's water to turn the mill. As responsiveness grows to the soul we become more whole and much less fatigued by things too mundane, that we get too caught up in. What can we do about people, places, and things? We can just enjoy the use of our eyes and ears to appreciate how it all has been made up. We can learn to concentrate in the emotional center a lifting, whereby we can catch that channel of love, joy, and hope; and holding long enough to it, begin to hear the *symphonic church* of the inner ear stretch itself into our auditory awareness.

To effloresce is part of the nature of man as it is of plants and animals. We hear the happy song of birds building a nest. The joy we hear is the peak growth of life purpose. Think of a saint, when she or he effloresced most compellingly. Or how your life might in this century here. The bloom comes when the energy to do so is given by the stems, the roots, the foliage, the light, and the soil.

To get to the center is done by staying there often. When the instinct for being centered has been cherished for a long time and the abilities are by no means overrated, there is balance and there is confidence. The centered ones do not feel sorry for themselves. Neither do they aggrandize themselves. They preserve an honest evaluation, and to these ones, reality is not a great paradox.

Going one step at a time: in actuality we are surprised how rapidly we can move along. The mind sees things to do. The emotions are eager, sometimes over-eager, and this can be a problem. The symptoms of a patience-deficiency are the duality of over-confidence and discouragement. Whatever the limiting factor is that we are most immediately encountering, the overcoming it needs to be acknowledged as our next step. The surprising swiftness of evolving the necessary attitudes and perspectives to be on your way comes through making the acknowledgment of the next limiting factor and allowing your joy and dedication to power you through it. A reflexive habit of live music therapy provides the timely acceleration. When the heart stays primed and the mind is not skipping steps or glossing over them, the evolution of plans and completing projects, of embarking on disciplines and following through with them, is a wondrously exciting business. Everything just seems to be there for you as it is needed; you feel so blessed and grateful for yourself and for the ones who are helping, with you, to make it all come true.

Letting circumstances dictate what we do is one way of avoiding responsibility for making decisions. And it is one way of making regrettable decisions. Effective decisions are made by establishing a core vision of life purpose and relating all the procedural steps of manifestation to this core vision. It is much better to face the difficulty of making the right decision than to abdicate our co-creatorship. "Going with the flow" mentality has its place, and squaring up objectively with our core vision has its place. Major decisions need to be free of inputs that are of extraneous or secondary significance.   Major decisions need to be fundamentally based on the primary significance of our core vision of life purpose. What is practically effective in the ultimate sense is what the will is willing to sustain. What the will is willing to sustain is a range of activity that is directly aligned with the core vision.

Decision making. Isn't this the area of life where the effort to grow spiritually really pays off? Not that we are all grown, not that the difficulty is all gone, but we can tell the how-we-approach of making a decision is improving. Spiritual growth begins to organize the qualities needed for good judgment. Spiritual growth is aware that good judgment does not just involve pacing around in the mind, but putting the mind at rest, because the desire has been born to let God speak. When a particular set of options is baffling, we can begin to approach the way we will go by keeping in mind that love is the beginning and the end and the middle of our journey.

Don't be so sure you know what to do. This strengthens the heart. But keep inhaling; this strengthens the lungs. If we use our hearts and lungs to advantage right livelihood will work out. We jot down our visions. We see how they interrelate. We still don't have it all figured out. But that is real, real okay, because the joy is real and the prospects are solid of something happening.

The value of experiencing human imperfection is to learn about the imperfection for the sake of seeing how it does not fit in the overall plan we wish to follow. The value is not in creating guilt. There is no value in that.

Keeping in mind that the creation of objective goals is precisely to further happiness, and not detract from it; then, if holding to your objectives is stressing you out, you know the way in which you are approaching them is dysfunctional. To functionally achieve objectives is to maintain a purity of logic and a purity of desire. There is no need for the ego to goad the lower self into toiling up the mountain. As a purity of logic and a purity of desire are maintained, the lower self is happily supplying its energy into the ascent. The realization in worldly terms of one's purpose can only be a reflection of what's inside. Those themes that reside within and abide naturally will sustain and guide the activities of getting the job done. Therefore, rule one in attaining objectives is to carry the quest along in a ceremonial way. Rule one means that impure forces of motivation do not further the good work we seek to accomplish. To keep the consciousness of attainment in a ceremonial way means to keep things light in the outward ego - reverent and playful. To get too heavy with oneself is to become dull, morose, and unreceptive. The goals are reached by following the clues and seeing the patterns clear. Heartfelt singing, chanting, and toning empower the ceremonial orientation.

There is a lot of fiction about deadlines which is not healthy; deadening is more like it. Which means for the sake of life we don't have to be jerked along by that massive thought form, which the anxiety that sickens modern man makes - to get it done and be admonished to do so. All of which only tends to detract us from the care we are trying to create for our work. When it becomes obvious that this project is not likely to get any better with more time, then, maybe, time is no longer the choice. The day comes for the product to arrive with a degree of finality. Leaking the good news never helped so much as the little battles won in self over the course of the creationary period. Doing our toning exercises and live music therapy is how these battles are won.

The straightest journey to any goal is along the pathway that is free of demanding and doubt. Impatience only lengthens the trip. What if it takes another year? Or ten years? If we are making progress we will get there. We will get what is coming to us. And the way it comes will be the way we want from the perspective of the moment when it is coming, and not before. Desire is holy. But we cannot fake the fulfillment of it. Desire is holy because it makes us whole. In making it happen we learn many things. The reason the soul works on these projects, our lives, is to help evolve the consciousness of mankind by getting the cosmic clues down into man's physical life.

We are like trees. We need time to grow, and to practice. Qualities come in time. In the meantime we gratefully apply ourselves to the job at hand of lifting up our song for the pleasure of God and the healing of creatures, ourselves included. We do not come to Paradise until we begin the journey there. To be in Paradise is to find that which we can do forever and keep doing it.

When we are hunting the prey of any definite goal, we make sure to pray, and make sure to be at peace when applying the strokes. The Earth has an axis, a lean to Her. She is leaning to reverence, and we, like she, need to be leaning that way too. All things to be wrought properly will be made with a ceremoniousness and without stress. To build anything well is not to endure in hell while it is built, but is to bring forth into the working sphere every day, the greater sphere, by peace, of heaven. Charging any task with oxygen, and with audible pure tones, has a way of getting the job done right.

Correctly speaking, life is a dance. Work is part of life, therefore work needs to be a dance. Work is a happy occasion when we participate in the dance of it. Elation is comprised of many things and work is not the least. Our work is our play. There is no *should* until there is a *can*, no span of doing joy cannot reach.

The night begins to fall. I may be finishing a section of work or welcoming the next with an intonation of the builder's chant. It is my way of giving a blessing on the work to come. Joy is the first word in the builder's chant which begins, "Joy to the Father, Joy to the Son." Whatever the project is, when the motivational picture in the builder's heart is very pure, guidance flows very freely into the work.

When there are many things we would like to do, but the perspective isn't quite complete or the right day hasn't arrived, and the whole syndrome looks like what passes as frustration; we look again, remembering work is to be a heightening of pleasure, and glimpse beyond the expectation of finding self in a state of annoyance, and surprise, see a state of serenity. We were aware of a tendency to become pensive or hasty. Moods are mainly things that have to do with rigid patterns of expecting this and this, and insisting on all manner of arbitrary things. We can just let the satisfaction come. No one likes demanding children, least of all God.

Now serenity may seem to many of us, because of our "tapes," to be elusive. But we can rehearse serenity just like we rehearse anxiety. Indeed, if we really consider who we are, it would seem more natural to rehearse serenity. We can sing a very peaceful song or one that reminds us to be at peace. If we have experienced being serene, then, when we are wondering what kind of mood to apply, we just trace back to the quality, call it forth to serve again. When circumstances seem to suggest anxiety, we can see how the mood of serenity is really our best choice. Intuitively, it does not feel like the right time for application of energy to a project at hand. So to keep in hand, we find it's much easier to be serene. Energy is conserved and we don't grate on the nerves of others. And when the alignment of the project comes together, the energy is ready to go and the follow through of application is a good fit.

Love for Nature is as promising a technique for liberation as any other. That which affords cosmic bliss to be *indwelling* is that which can be practiced to advantage. True nature lovers are yogis. They are appropriately ascetic because they are appropriately aesthetic. The singing nature lover gathers in this affection of genuine devotion for the mountain or ocean or stream or whatever and attracts liberating vibrations from the Heart of Creation to blend into what, in turn, may be sent out to the world as a transmitting of bliss because the direct appeal and appreciation is to God. For the musician to reach her brothers and sisters, she must first be reached by Spirit. The commitment of a relationship to Mother Nature that is without deficit, is the key to the magic that can heal a culture.

If enough energy is supplied things change. At Iguazu Falls in South America, 1700 tons of water fall every second. The roar, the spectacle, the misty atmosphere, have a definite energizing effect on the people who come to be here in the presence of this natural phenomenon. Many people have remarked that being on a certain mountain has changed them. Or in a certain canyon, or through contact with other creatures, like whales. The appearance of clouds, trees, the way of a dawn or a storm, and so forth - all can penetrate productively into the receptive person. Being changed does not have to be a collision. The impact can be gentle. When certain, subtler parts of consciousness are awakened, the change is none the less profound for it being gentle.

The elements of nature are the design of Spirit and the evolution of a person's awareness of this reality is highly pertinent to self healing. This might be termed the passive mode of the dynamics of change. In the active mode the energy is supplied, to some extent, by the people involved. We can create healings. We can work together. We can sustain a lot of effort towards a worthy goal. We can experience very comforting culminations of building patience, kindness, and devotion. If enough energy is channeled into a great challenge, seemingly impossible things do occur. The more people grow in Spirit, the more pure energy they have to work with in giving of themselves. How much love can fill up you being is directly related to what kind of live music you can sustain outwardly to comfort yourself and others. This is a very precise relationship of cause and effect. Love increases willingness to serve. Willingness to serve increases ability to serve. The charge of upliftment works to assist in areas of *body karma* release and often times contributes to a sudden and powerful transformation.

Why bother to make emotional changes and practice spiritual attunements? Because life gets boring if we don't. Stagnation just isn't all that interesting. No matter how often we get away to interesting events and places, if we refuse to enter new spaces of character, the dullness never leaves.

We have got all the information, many times over again, to invalidate that which is not working and validate that which is. If our *trip* is not coming alive enough for us, it is not because there is not enough information. It is because there is not enough integrity. Not enough integration. The flaw is in the feelings and the emotions. The positive effort of the heart is being withheld. If we feel like we are moving in slow motion, if indeed, moving at all; then we reread the bottom line - the positive effort of the heart is being withheld.

Conditions change if enough energy is brought forward to change them. Almost anything and everything is likely to work when the positive effort of the heart is not withheld. The initiative simply amounts to not withholding. The hilarity of what we do to circumvent the inevitable is really a sad thing. The power to change irreversibly is irreversibly in any one moment, a potential to be tapped, but which is left untouched because of the madness of mediocrity. Man procrastinates with the inevitablities of evolution because he is afraid to reach out and be helped so that he can be of excellence. There is nothing more than this to say, to know, to ponder, of the way - Life will redound to you.

LMT/APT is a growth process based on repetition. When we find something that works we will keep working it and we will follow as the door opens. Our ears, it is often said, are the doorways of the soul. Hearing is the art of patience, of waiting to be called by the soul. We start to hear more things, and a finer quality of things, because we keep listening heartwise for the sounds of God and the sounds of God begin transmitting. Healing by bliss becomes our way and we have found something that really satisfies. We have discovered an experiential yoga, and the level of communion increases experience by experience. By doing our LMT's and APT's religiously, as needed, in the directly natural and spontaneous way of living our life, we greatly assist the lifting work of Spirit. We can heal in privacy. We can share it. The Truth is in all of us and It can arise if we will allow It to happen and assist It to happen.

For information on seminars and trainings here at Live Music Therapy Retreat Center and around the country, please write to:

Live Music Therapy
Star Rt. Box 379-A
Burnet, Texas 78611

Additional copies of this book may be ordered from the Live Music Therapy Press. Send $5.95 for each desired copy. Texas residents, please add appropriate sales tax.